# 10 GOOD REASONS TO BE A CATHOLIC

## A Teenager's Guide to the Church

**Jim Auer**

Liguori

ONE LIGUORI DRIVE
LIGUORI MO 63057-9999

Imprimi Potest:
Stephen T. Palmer, C.SS.R.
Provincial, St. Louis Province
The Redemptorists

Imprimatur:
+ Edward J. O'Donnell
Vicar General, Archdiocese of St. Louis

ISBN 978-0-89243-271-4
Library of Congress Card Number 87-80988

Liguori Publications, a nonprofit corporation, is an apostolate of
the Redemptorists. To learn more about the Redemptorists, visit
Redemptorists.com.

To order, call 1-800-325-9521
www.liguori.org

Cover design by Christine Kraus

# Table of Contents

# 1
# Why Be a
# Catholic Today?

How do TV or the movies portray religion? Think about it! Whenever they want to bring up the subject of religion, they write a script that calls for a priest or a Sister. When the media bigwigs need a character to officially represent religion, they call on a Catholic.

This isn't a new trend, either. Artworks, plays, and novels have done it for centuries. In the movies it's been going on at least since 1938 when Pat O'Brien played a kindly priest in the movie *Angels With Dirty Faces.* Ask your grandparents about that one! Then there was Bing Crosby's 1944 Oscar-winning portrayal of a priest in *Going My Way* (which also won the Academy Award for Best Film). The devil's opponents, when he possessed Linda Blair in *The Exorcist,* were two priests.

Television has had more than its share of stories about priests and Sisters. Some, like Merlin Olsen's Father Murphy and Peter Falk's Father Noah "Hardstep" Rivers, have been the main character in the program. Countless others have played supporting roles, but there can be no doubt that Catholic priests and Sisters appear as characters in films and on TV programs much more often than religious leaders from any other Church or religious denomination.

It also works in reverse. When the media needs a Representative-of-Religion-Gone-Wrong, the choice again is usually a priest or a Sister. More than one movie and plenty of TV programs have told the story of priests and Sisters who have fallen in love, broken their vows, inflicted pain and suffering on others, or been involved in financial misdeeds.

Why do they always pick Catholic figures to represent religion? Good question.

Is it that most priests and Sisters dress differently? Well, representatives of other faiths sometimes dress distinctively too. Is it that Catholicism is the major Christian religion in terms of numbers? (More than seventeen percent of the world population and twenty-two percent of the population of the United States are Catholic.)

Or is there a general, unspoken feeling that somehow the Catholic faith is "the real thing" when it comes to religion?

## Why are you Catholic?

All this makes interesting speculation, but there are more important, personal questions to consider. For example, how do *you* see your own Catholic faith? What images come to mind when you hear the phrase "the Catholic Church"? Why are you a Catholic today? Do you feel committed to the Church or do you sense that you are on the fringe? Do you think you'll still be a Catholic ten or twenty years from now?

It's not likely that you are a Catholic because you chose the Catholic faith after a long, personal search. You are probably Catholic because at least one of your parents, if not both, is a Catholic, and that parent saw to it that you were baptized in the Catholic Church when you were still very young.

Some people feel that infant baptism is a terrible injustice on the part of the Catholic Church, as though this practice is an attempt to hold a helpless kid a lifelong captive of the faith. But the same situation is found among people of many religious communities. Hundreds of thousands of young people were "born Methodist" or "born Baptist" or "born Hindu" and have been members of those communities ever since, whether they were officially baptized or initiated into the faith, or whether they just grew up in the faith under the influence of their parents.

Sooner or later, however, you're going to need a better reason for being and remaining Catholic than simply because Mom, Dad, relatives, or friends are Catholic. When you make the choice to personally live your life as a Catholic and follow the laws and practices of the Catholic Church, then you can call yourself a *mature* believer. But if you want to find those better reasons, it's going to take a little work and study and thought.

Right now your image and impressions of the Catholic faith and the institution called the Catholic Church have probably come from a rather limited number of people: your parents, the priests and Sisters you've met, teachers in Catholic schools or religious education programs, classmates and friends, and other members of your parish. You have probably also learned about the Church from some of the things you have read, like the Bible and religion textbooks. Retreats, Sunday sermons, and other religious services have also taught you something about the Church.

Sometimes this has resulted in a wonderfully accurate representation of the whole Church and sometimes not. Some kids are "raised Catholic" mainly because their grandmothers would have "raised the roof" if they didn't go to church — or because somebody figured there'd be fewer drugs and higher achievement scores in a Catholic school.

Situations like that can give the impression that there isn't a very good, genuinely religious reason to stick with the Catholic faith over any other.

## Looking things over

When you're "born into" one Church and begin looking at others, there are a couple of attitudes you want to avoid.

One goes like this: "All the religious truth in the universe belongs to our religion. All other religions worship false gods or at least have beliefs that are really quite confused. If they don't straighten out, God may very likely waste them in hell — or if they get into heaven, they won't be nearly as high up and happy as *WE* are."

Unfortunately, many people formerly thought this way — including some Catholics who were so convinced that Catholicism was the only road to God that they weren't very charitable toward other groups of believers. Some people still act this way, particularly some fundamentalist Christians who believe solely in their literal interpretation of the Bible. They tend to look upon Catholics, Episcopalians, and Lutherans as hopelessly confused and misguided practicers of semi-superstition who are quite probably headed for hell.

The second mistake goes like this: "What difference does it

7

make what religion you belong to? They're practically all the same anyway. As long as you don't hurt people and you live a good life, that's all that counts."

Usually that's a cop out, an excuse for not thinking, for going along with whatever seems easy, or for not having any faith at all. Sometimes, however, it's an overreaction. We're trying so hard to avoid giving an "I'm right and you're wrong" impression that we end up saying, "It doesn't make any difference."

But what you believe *does* make a difference. If you believe that Jesus was the greatest teacher of all times and the model of Christian living, then you'll look for a Christian faith community *that upholds and presents Jesus' message as completely and faithfully as possible.*

For me, that community of faithful believers is found in the Catholic Church. It's not that I'm ignorant of other Christians and their churches and traditions or that I judge them to be totally wrong. Nor do I believe the Catholic Church and all its leaders and members are perfect. There have been times when I have been bored by the Church, confused by the Church, and angry with the Church.

That's OK. That sort of thing has been going on for a long time. Even Peter and Paul had their differences. As for being bored, read the story in Acts 20:7-12 about a kid named Eutychus. This guy got so tired of listening to Paul preach that he dozed off and fell out of a third-story window — and Paul was an awfully good preacher!

Anyway, I'm still Catholic — the way I was born. But it's by choice now. I know my reasons for choosing my Church.

You need to know yours.

## Things to consider

Some people are impressed by historical evidence. For example, the Catholic Church can trace its leadership from the present pope all the way back to Peter. That doesn't mean every pope has been terrific any more than all United States' presidents have been the equal of Washington or Lincoln. It does show, however, that the Catholic faith is not a strange new idea on the religious horizon.

Others are impressed by results of the Catholic effort over the centuries in response to the command of Jesus to care for and love one another. More hospitals (6,475 worldwide), orphanages (6,393), homes for the handicapped and aged, schools, and universities (all due to the tremendous effort and sacrifice of individual Catholics) have been set up and operated by the Catholic Church than by any other organization, religious or secular.

For many others the reason for their choice to become or remain Catholic is found in worship. Catholics believe that when Jesus said "This is my Body" and "Do this in remembrance of me" at the Last Supper, he meant exactly that. Catholics believe in the Real Presence of Jesus in the Eucharist — that Jesus chose to be *physically present* among us under the signs of bread and wine, and that he gave priests the power to transform the bread and wine into his Body and Blood. That presence of the Lord in our worship is something of vital importance to Catholics.

Many others respect the fact that the Catholic Church has a clear authority structure. Jesus did not, after all, drift up to heaven and leave things on earth up in the air. Nor did he leave behind a discussion group where "whatever you wanna do" was the name of the game. He left people in charge: Peter and the apostles. Authority isn't always the most pleasant and welcome thing in life, but without it things often don't ever really get settled or done. That leadership is what unites Catholics all over the world into one spirit and body (which is what Jesus wanted in the first place).

## Is everybody happy?

Now think back to that image or feeling you have when you see or hear "Catholic Church."

If there's a sort of a blank, then you have a blank to fill and that can be kind of exciting.

If you get a good feeling, a proud feeling, about being part of the Catholic tradition, great! After all, you're allowed to — in fact, you're supposed to — feel right and good about your beliefs. (Of course, that doesn't mean you have the right to put down someone else's religious beliefs.)

If you get a negative image or feeling, try to find out where it comes from. Is it based on the whole picture of the Church — from Jesus down to the present — or is it just a couple of things (or people) that bug you?

Sometimes people expect a perfect-or-nothing relationship with the Church. They figure anything that claims to represent Jesus should be perfect in all ways and make everybody happy all the time.

That's not humanly possible.

Jesus said he would be with us until the end of time. He never said he'd make all Christians perfect before the end of time, including those people who "run the Church." Remember, it was Peter, the very person Jesus chose to take charge, who denied Jesus and said "I don't even know the man" three times.

As for making everybody happy and in agreement, *even Jesus didn't do that!* If you're expecting that from our Church leadership, you're expecting something Jesus never claimed, promised, or delivered. The gospel message isn't going to hit everybody with the soft caress of a gentle breeze. When you have regular old human beings delivering that message, it can get even harder to accept.

But that's how God chose to do things — and it's probably a pretty smart idea to accept his plan just the way he gave it. (I'm willing to give almost anyone in the universe some good, needed advice, but I don't think it's too great an idea to try to coach God.)

Why Catholic?

For me, there are lots of reasons. And it doesn't mean I think the Catholic Church is perfect or that other Churches are wasting their time. Two Sundays ago I attended an evening worship and song service at a nearby Baptist church. The Spirit was . . . well, *WOW* is the only accurate word to describe it. It was prayerful, powerful, and uplifting. I felt enriched by that service, but the Catholic Church is still my Church.

You need to find your own reasons for being Catholic. They don't have to be different from anyone else's, but they do have to be yours — and you have to truly believe in them.

The reasons are there. I hope you find them.

# 2
# Measuring
# Your Faith Quotient

How strong is your faith? What do you really believe? For centuries, people have been trying to categorize different types of faith. Now, thanks to modern technology, we have the "Unicorn, Unicycle, Cranberries, Water, and Loch Ness Monster test." In less than ten minutes, in the comfort of your own home, you can find out where you stand in this whole faith business.

OK, so maybe our test isn't the finest triumph of modern technology or theology. But it *can* be helpful in assessing your faith. Let's give it a shot.

## Check it out

*Unicorns* don't exist, but a lot of people like them. Beautiful, even inspiring stories have been written about unicorns. Unicorn posters decorate walls all over the country. Some people look at faith in the same way they see unicorns: It's imaginary but it does inspire nice thoughts.

The *Loch Ness monster* is a creature that may or may not exist. There's some evidence but it's not conclusive. Most people find the idea interesting, but they don't pour their lives into the search, even if they believe it's real. If the monster's there, fine. If not, that's OK too. In either case it has very little to do with them or the way they live their lives. For some people, faith is like that. "Maybe it's real, maybe it's not," or "There's probably a God but, like the Loch Ness monster, so what?"

*Unicycles* are definitely real. Nobody disagrees about that. You can even buy one if you want. Many people figure riding a unicycle might be a kick if they learned how. But it's not worth it to them. It takes too much time and makes you look sort of different in public. Some people see faith like that. It is a waste of time that costs too much money and limits one's freedom.

For others, faith is like *cranberries.* Cranberries are usually something you want a little of now and then, often for the sake of tradition, like at Thanksgiving. But they're not something most people want to have once a day or even once a week. Faith is like that for some folks. It's absolutely essential, at least in small doses, for weddings, funerals, Christmas, and Easter. The rest of the time it doesn't seem too necessary.

Then again, faith is like *water* to some people. Sometimes pure water is the most delicious, satisfying thing you can possibly swallow. You'd choose it over anything else. Other times, straight water seems a little dull. Either way, it's part of everything you drink. You wouldn't dream of trying to live without it.

We could probably extend our list of examples, but I think there's enough here to work with. Where's *your* faith? It's worth checking out.

The purpose isn't to locate yourself on a scale from wonderful to rotten. (If you're at a Loch Ness monster or unicycle stage, it doesn't mean God sees you as a decayed anchovy on the great pizza of life.) The purpose is to understand where you stand so you can decide whether or not you want to stay there.

## Faith is faith

The first thing we ought to say about faith is that it's *faith.* That's not an amazing discovery; I'm not claiming a twentieth-century religious breakthrough. But it's not a dumb statement either. In fact, it needs to be restated every now and then because we keep trying to make faith into something else.

A virus hangs around in our religious bloodstream promoting the idea that if religion is genuine somebody should be able to explain it and prove it and make it as easy to see as picking out the good guys and bad guys on a television program. Faith will never be like that. If you could prove every speck of it, you'd have religious algebra or something — but not faith.

Having questions about faith or about correct Church teachings isn't bad or dumb. Asking "How do we know . . . ?" is pretty natural. It's just that when we're dealing with God there'll be times when we come up with a blank, sometimes known as a mystery. There are lots of things I want to find out when I make it to that Great Racquetball Court in the Sky because I sure don't understand them down here. But if all these mysteries could be proven and explained simply, we wouldn't be talking about faith.

Not everything about faith is a completely wild shot in the dark, though. For example, there is one rather believable and logical argument for the existence of God based on the "order of the universe." Basically it says that if you study scientific data about how this whole cosmic ball park fits together, the idea that it all just fell into place by itself and by accident is ridiculous. The conclusion has to be "Somebody bigger and smarter than me did this! There must be a God!"

While this is not an absolute proof, it makes a lot of sense to me and to many people, but not to everybody. Some people listen and genuinely say, "I don't agree."

## The search for faith

For the most part, I don't think you can argue with people and convince them that there is a God or that they should practice their faith. Statements showing how our Christian faith is "the logical way to go" or even "the smart way to go" undoubtedly win some people over, or at least make them think about what you have said.

More commonly, I believe, people discover or rediscover faith because of big empty spots inside themselves, in their lives. After a while they realize something odd: All the money, pleasure, and creature comforts that were supposed to make life worth living and bring happiness aren't doing it.

Unlimited parties aren't doing it. Scrambling and scraping to get ahead in school or in business is challenging but often leaves you asking, "Why am I doing this?" Strange as it may seem to some, it's possible to have a spot on the starting lineup, a straight-A average, a circle of admirers, a built-in pool in the backyard, a Rolls Royce in the driveway, and gourmet food on the table — and still ask, "Is this all there is to life?"

It's not only possible, it happens a lot!

## Joy through faith

Look around you and ask, "Who's happy?" *Who is really happy?*

Is it the people who have surrounded themselves with mountains of this world's metal and plastic? Is it the people who say "Get all you can get because when you're gone, it's all over"?

Or is it the people of faith who look beyond metal and plastic?

How many people of genuine faith do you know who are positively miserable . . . who walk around griping, dissatisfied, full of bitterness and turmoil, always wishing things were different and better?

I'm willing to bet not many.

The human heart has a great instinct for what's real. We're genuinely happy only when we're dealing with real stuff. And the real stuff of life goes beyond what we see on the surface of this world.

A long time ago, Saint Augustine said the same thing in different words: "You have made us for yourself, O God, and our hearts are restless until they rest in you." You can mess around with dozens of high-tech ways to turn on, but only God can make you happy.

## Faith makes sense

The crazy thing about faith is that at first it seems not to make sense — but once you've found it, it's exactly the one thing that *does* make sense out of everything.

For example, people who don't believe in God see disappointments as rotten breaks that leave them feeling cheated and hassled and angry. With faith, disappointment and suffering can actually be viewed as God challenging you to try something more and better; God leading you away from something harmful; God trying to teach you something you wouldn't learn if everything went smoothly.

Without faith, much of life is just plain boring and a waste of time: Get this done; get that out of the way so that you have time to do the "fun" things in life. Interruptions in your schedule of Really Important Stuff That Makes Life Enjoyable can frustrate the heck out of you.

Your little brother can't find a toy, for example, and you "waste" a half hour trying to find it. Faith won't transform the search into a fascinating, thrill-filled adventure, but it does tell you that the time wasn't wasted. In fact, that half hour might be the most significant chunk of time you've spent all day.

## Invisible dimension

Many people are fascinated by the concept of a twilight zone — the idea of another dimension surrounding us into which we cross over now and then.

Well, for a long time God has been telling us, "Yes, there is another dimension! It's often invisible but it's real. It's around and inside everything you see, including yourself. There's more than what you see on the outside."

Sometimes we sort of yawn about it. We buy those sensational national newspapers and read articles with headlines like "Top Scientist Reveals Evidence of the Universe's Invisible Dimension" and think, "Wow, that's fascinating." When we hear God's word about the invisible dimension, the Kingdom to come in this created universe, sometimes we say, "That's just that religion stuff."

How do you contact this other dimension? Secret spells? Psychic travel? Magic words?

That's it! Two magic words, "I believe!"

These words aren't always easy to say and really mean. Sometimes they might stick in your throat because you think, "Yeah, I can say I believe, but do I really?" You don't want to be phony. Maybe you even *want* to believe, wish you could believe . . . but you don't know how to go about it.

The Gospel of Mark tells about a man in exactly that situation. And he came up with a terrific, beautiful, honest prayer about it. You can find it in chapter 9, verse 14. Slightly reworded, his prayer goes like this: "Lord, I do believe . . . sort of. I'd like to believe more strongly, but I need your help to do that."

He's *asking for faith!* Great idea. You're allowed to do that, you know. Sometimes people think they have to be already filled with one hundred percent pure, high-potency, anti-doubt, made-in-heaven faith *before* they can approach God.

Nobody ever said that, including God!

# 3
# The Mansion with the Cool Old Stuff

Old things can be really neat or really bad. Some old things are neat for many reasons — sometimes precisely *because* they are old. Of course, not everything old is good. You could make a couple of categories: GOS (Gross Old Stuff) and COS (Cool Old Stuff). Under GOS we'd have things like month-old pieces of leftover pizza in the back of the refrigerator. Under COS we'd have things like 1966 Mustangs and fragile, irreplaceable Christmas ornaments that hung on your great-grandmother's tree.

For the next few pages, let's consider some of the COS that is part of the Catholic Church and our Christian faith tradition.

## The Catholic Church

You might say that we Catholics live in an old mansion called the Catholic Church. (Two thousand years definitely qualifies as old, and the Church can be described as a very large and complex structure, so it also qualifies as a mansion.) Of course, the Church is not like an old mansion that has been preserved with nothing but objects from some bygone era. It's more like a mansion that has undergone several extensive remodelings and additions. And, very important, it is not a mansion that only a few special people can live in. It's a mansion open to anybody who wants to live there. There's room for everybody.

Picture an old mansion that has had the heating system updated and the kitchen and bathrooms remodeled for modern living. The plumbing and wiring have been redone. The old carriage house has been expanded into a three-car garage. The library has shelves and shelves of valuable ancient books side-by-side with a computer and data processing center. You have the beauty of the old with the convenience of the new.

Now that's the way it is with the Catholic Church today: a mixture of Neat New Stuff and Cool Old Stuff. We sometimes call the COS "traditions." People who have grown up and spent their entire life in the old mansion have probably grown so used to it that they fail to appreciate it.

This chapter will allow you to take a new look at some of the Cool Old Stuff in our Catholic mansion. Notice the word "some." We have only a few pages and this is a very old, very complex mansion, so we'll call this our Quickie Tour.

## A look around

Some people might expect our mansion to be rather bare, an assortment of dull, stark rooms where you're supposed to tune out the world, forget you have a body with five senses, and concentrate only on spiritual stuff.

Not so! In fact, just the opposite is true. Our Catholic mansion is positively full of things designed to turn on the senses. People who see religion as mainly a mental trip haven't visited the Catholic mansion or, if they have, did not look close enough.

Start with candles. Terrific things, candles. If you haven't done so lately, light one and look at it, preferably in a darkened room. There's something very elemental and magnetic about a candle flame.

Candles are lit for every Mass and for many other Church services. In our worship, candles aren't just neat-looking, semi-mysterious sources of light. They are symbols of Jesus whom we follow, Jesus who is the Light of our life, Jesus who lights our path through the darkness.

The most important use of a candle comes on Holy Saturday evening at the Easter Vigil. In this service we focus on the central candle of every Catholic Church, the Paschal Candle. For a few wonderful moments during that vigil service we are enveloped in darkness except for the Paschal Candle — which then gives light to the small candle each person holds. Liturgy by candlelight. Maybe we should do it more often.

In the mansion with the cool old stuff, should we celebrate by using plain old black and white? No way! If we open our eyes, we'll see a feast of color. Think about the celebration of the Mass, the Liturgy of the Eucharist. The priest's vestments change colors with the liturgical season and, in many churches, so do the banners on the walls and the cloth that drapes across or in front of the altar.

These color changes aren't just made for the sake of variety. Each color *says* something. Gold or white tells of glory, joy, and happiness. Purple is used for Lent, the season of penance. Red reminds us of the blood shed by the martyrs for the faith. Green is a hopeful color. In Advent many churches use purple, but others have started to use a deep blue, like the color of the sky just before sunrise, to signify the Church's waiting for Christ's coming at Christmas.

Besides the sensory magic of light and dark and color, we capture the sensory magic of water in our Catholic traditions. There is water for making the Sign of the Cross at the entrances of our churches, water that welcomes us at Baptism, and the sprinkling of water that accompanies many special ceremonies. Some churches even have a small waterfall so you can hear and see and feel water in a very real way.

There's something wonderful about water, just as there is about colors and candles. But this isn't just any old water. The water used in our ceremonies has been blessed, so we call it *holy water.* It's special and it's different.

Now some folks confuse holy water with superstition. No way! Holy water and rabbit's feet have nothing in common. But to prevent confusion, we'd better say something about *sacramentals* since many Church traditions center around them.


## Blessings and faith

Things that have been blessed by God (like water, candles, the ashes we use on Ash Wednesday) are called "sacramentals." The blessing makes them special, but it doesn't make them magical. You don't get an admission ticket to heaven by lighting a few hundred candles in church. If you took a fifteen-minute shower in holy water, you'd turn out cleaner but not necessarily any holier.

A blessed object is like a charged battery; there's power in it. The power in the battery doesn't make anything happen, however, unless something is plugged into it. The same is true with sacramentals.

What is it that has to be plugged in for the power to be released? *Faith,* simple faith in a God who has chosen often to speak and work through the things of our world rather than asking us to tune them out.

Faith in sacramentals is not a matter of "I'll light this candle and douse myself with holy water. That will wipe out all the times I've pushed my brother around, which I don't intend to stop doing because it's too much fun." That's trying to play games with God. It doesn't work and it gives sacramentals a bad image.

There's a wealth of things designed to turn on the senses and turn our minds and hearts to God. Besides what we've already mentioned, there's incense (wonderful stuff, unless you're allergic to it), medals, rosaries, statues, pictures, and stained-glass windows. The list could go on and on. In chapter five of this book we'll take a fuller look at sacramentals and how they can help us see Christ in our life and draw closer to God.


## The Real Presence

Can you pray anywhere, anytime? Sure, it's possible and recommended. Some places, however, are better than others for most people. Most people probably find it easier to pray by a lakeshore at sunrise than standing on a ladder as they clean crud out of the gutter, for example. Even though you can talk to God anywhere, churches make great places to really get into the conversation. Surrounded by sacramentals like crucifixes and stained-glass windows, we can sense more clearly the presence of God.

For one thing, in our Catholic tradition we see a church not simply as a place where people gather for worship. We literally believe that

Jesus is present there, in the form of the eucharistic bread, the consecrated hosts kept in the tabernacle. Officially this is called the teaching of the Real Presence.

In the past, some folks put more attention on the presence of Jesus in the tabernacle than on the main reason for his presence: to be shared by all believers during the sacrificial meal of the Mass. In putting the emphasis back where it belongs, we may have forgotten how neat it is to walk into church and know that, in a very special and real way, *Jesus is truly present!*

If you haven't done it recently, and if there is a Catholic church you can visit, take advantage of that. OK, so it takes guts to walk into a church by yourself when you don't have to, like on a Wednesday afternoon. But try it — particularly if there's something you'd like to talk over with the Lord.

In older Catholic language this tradition is called "a visit to the Blessed Sacrament." I like that term. Friends do like to *visit,* don't they?

## Catholic body language

Our belief that Jesus is present in the church is the reason we genuflect or bow toward the tabernacle when we enter or leave church — another neat custom. It's an old one but it fits perfectly with our contemporary interest in body language and getting physical.

There are many times when our Catholic tradition calls for body language. The most basic, the one most of us learned first, is the Sign of the Cross. Talk about putting the basics in a small package! We believe that God is a Trinity of persons who love us: the Father, the Son, and the Spirit. We believe that the Son, who became Jesus, saved us through his death on the Cross and his rising. It's all there, in words and in body language, in the Sign of the Cross. Try it in a brand-new way sometime soon. Concentrate on making your physical motion an act of "I believe."

Standing, sitting, kneeling, singing, listening, praying aloud — they are all signs of our relationship with God. Can you think of other types of Catholic body language?

## God's Hall of Fame

At the end of the movie *Close Encounters of the Third Kind,* a stark statement appeared on the screen: *"We Are Not Alone!"*

One of our strongest Catholic traditions says the same thing. There are other people in this cosmic ball game, and we can communicate with them. This is the basis for our tradition of honoring the saints. (The official term for this is the Mystical Body of Christ — a neat phrase when you think about it.)

It doesn't mean you can call Saint Peter or your recently deceased great-grandmother on some earth-to-heaven super long-distance system. In fact, like many "heavenly" things, we don't completely understand it. But we do believe in a mysterious, mystical (but very real) connectedness between folks still here on planet Earth and those who have died and entered eternal life.

It is quite possible to talk to the saints. In earthly life some of them did marvelously spiritual things, had special interests and talents, or went through experiences that gave them insights we can use. So we ask certain ones to pray for us, guide us, and strengthen us in certain things.

*Saints don't take the place of God.* They're more like the veteran quarterback who's already made the Hall of Fame helping out the rookie who's trying to become a great quarterback.


## Further explorations

It's a complex mansion, this Catholic Church, filled with lots of Cool Old Stuff. There is also plenty of room in the mansion for Neat New Stuff to exist side-by-side with the Cool Old Stuff.

It takes both. If you think only of the old stuff, you get narrow and dried up and unable to see the Church as it really is today. If you think only of the new stuff, you float around disconnected, with no roots, unable to see the beauty of our traditions.

Check into some of our Catholic Cool Old Stuff. You might find a lot of it like your grandmother's recipes: They may be old but they sure are good.

# 4
# Sacraments:
# Fantastic Realities

Fantasy literature is big stuff these days. Your school library may be filled with Tolkien and Madeleine L'Engle and other good writers of fantasy. If you browse through a bookstore, you'll see one trilogy after another, or whole series such as Piers Anthony's *Xanth* stories.

These fantastic fantasy stories are filled with ghosts, goblins, dragons, and other unusual creatures who manage to become involved in some rather unreal, scary situations. While goblins are bad enough, a husky troll in a really foul mood is worse. Occasionally a dragon appears in a fantasy story. Now that's high-tech danger. When a dragon exhales on you at fifteen hundred degrees centigrade, you're history. And dragons carry grudges against practically everybody. They probably didn't get enough loving in their childhood.

Fortunately there is good news in these fantasy stories too. They contain a rather large stockpile of spells and magic crystals and wizards to combat the evil forces.

Here's one fantasy story you may not have come across in your reading since it's brand new! In its own way it also has something very important to say about the Catholic faith.

---

## A JOURNEY THROUGH EARTHWOOD

Deeper and deeper into the dense, dark green of Earthwood the path led them. Sometimes it was wide enough that two people could walk side-by-side, sometimes so narrow that it hardly seemed a path at all but only a few inches of murky space between walls of bark and leaves.

The three young men, Vopalt, Skan, and Blesivor, and two young women, Rea and Irin, trudged on, scarcely remembering how long they had been traveling. It seemed eons ago, when they were much, much younger, that they had begun a journey on behalf of the Master. Now the hills seemed higher, the ravines steeper, the forest darker, and the direction of their journey more confusing.

They stopped for the evening where the path widened into a soft grassy area surrounded by bronzeberries and herbs.

"This is stupid," Skan announced with disgust. "A journey through a forest like this is not for ordinary people like us."

"Nobody said it would be like this," agreed Rea, leaning against a purple-barked coryx tree. "We need . . . I don't know. We need *something.*"

"This is just great!" Blesivor countered sarcastically. "Okay, folks, let's all look around for something that can help us, okay? Anybody see a 'something' sitting around here?"

"Wrong place," boomed a voice as deep as a canyon from behind Rea. She jumped to her feet, dove for cover, and landed in a heap several yards away from the coryx tree. It was the tree that had spoken.

"Are we in the wrong place?" asked Vopalt rather timidly, for it was a very powerful looking tree.

"Your vision is in the wrong place," said the coryx tree. "You are looking around you, outside you. Look within . . . and remember."

## The Crystal Waterfall

The five stood looking rather blankly, first down at themselves and then at each other.

"Do you remember the Crystal Waterfall?" the tree continued.

"We know it happened. It's difficult to remember," Irin said.

"And difficult to understand," added Rea, recovering from her fright.

"Then listen. When you stood beneath the Waterfall, you were changed. You are no longer what you seem to be. What do you see on the outside?"

"Five confused, discouraged people lost in Earthwood," Vopalt answered after a moment of honest thought.

"That is what you *seem* to be . . . not what you *are!*" the coryx tree explained.

"Then what are we?"

"Trail diviners . . . adventurers. . . . When you stood beneath the Crystal Waterfall, the Master touched you and gave you a vision and special powers you haven't begun to realize! He changed each of you and brought you a share in his power and a special sense of oneness with each other. The goal of your journey through Earthwood is already inside you."

They closed their eyes and looked within themselves, then opened their eyes and looked around. It was the same grassy clearing, but without knowing quite how to put it into words, they seemed to *understand* the purpose of their journey a bit better. On the far side of the clearing, the path leading onward into the darkness looked less discouraging.

"Never tell yourselves you will not find the way through Earthwood. When you cannot see the way, it will find you. That is the Master's promise. You are chosen. You are not merely what you seem."

There was a pause in the gathering darkness, and the five intrepid adventurers thought the tree had ceased speaking, but it left a final message.

"You must find the Mountain of Wind and Fire. There you will receive . . . "

The booming voice of the purple-barked coryx tree trailed off to a bare whisper and they heard only the black-green silence around them, and they slept.

## The Great Eagle

They had traveled an hour or so the next morning when a great eagle came swooshing to a perch above their heads and peered down at them quizzically.

"You journey more confidently than before," the eagle said in a raspy but friendly voice.

"Yes, but how do you know?" asked Vopalt.

"Oh, I've seen you now and then," the eagle answered. "This is one of my favorite parts of Earthwood. I fly over here frequently."

"Then you must know the way to the Mountain of Wind and Fire!" Vopalt said.

"Of course I do, but are you quite certain you want to go there?"

"Why wouldn't we?"

"One does not go to the Mountain of Wind and Fire without . . . but that is not my concern. That is yours and the Master's."

"The Master? Will we see the Master at the Mountain of Wind and Fire?" Rea asked, suddenly very excited.

"See? See? Well now, there are many ways of seeing. So very many ways. You perhaps . . . but again, that is not mine to say. Now, directions, directions. From the air, of course, it's quite simple. From the ground it's a little more difficult. After the path has taken you over the second ridge you will see a small meadow to your right. Cross it and then . . . "

## One and Many Ways

The way to the top of the mountain was one way and many ways. Although they traveled together, Vopalt and Rea struggled to surmount steep cliffs that were at once scary and exciting. Skan nearly sprinted along a grassy path that carried him painlessly upward. Irin's way was lined with huge fallen trees, beautiful but deadly razor rocks, and spider shrubs that crept toward her and tried to ensnare her from behind. Blesivor arrived without knowing quite how he had gotten there.

When they got to the mountaintop, Vopalt began by saying, "We come seeking . . . " He was interrupted by a thunderclap and then a low rumbling roar that grew louder and somewhat higher in pitch. Rea heard it too, and then they realized that the roar was a great wind that began to swirl wildly around the mountaintop and envelop them. They heard the wind and felt the wind and saw the wind and for a moment became one with the wind. When it left them at last, they had no words for what had happened, but they knew that what began at the Crystal Waterfall had been completed on the Mountain of Wind and Fire.

Irin and Skan did not notice the wind, but they saw fire rising out of the earth. It was a silent fire that surrounded them and entered them. It did not feel like fire at all, but rather like a gentle rain that fell on them and into and through them. They stood with eyes closed and faces uplifted, feeling the gentle rainfire.

Blesivor stood and waited to see or feel something. He knew he was standing on the Mountain of Wind and Fire, but he could not tell if he saw or heard or felt anything different. In the end he did not think that he had.

## Alone in Earthwood

On the way down the mountain and for days afterward, Blesivor was upset and angry, especially at Vopalt, who kept talking about his experience of the wind. Early one afternoon shortly after lunch, Vopalt began speaking again and the smile on his face was more than Blesivor could stand. His fingers curled around a fist-sized rock. He stood up, brought his arm back, and hurled the rock at Vopalt. The rock struck Vopalt on the side of his face and knocked him down. Then Blesivor fled alone through the thick forest.

For days Blesivor trudged through Earthwood alone, having no particular place to go. He tried to keep heading in the same direction as his former companions, although he didn't know why. He woke one morning and was so depressed he didn't feel like moving an inch — so he didn't until a large speckled rabbit took a long leap and landed on him. Then Blesivor moved quite a bit — and quickly!

"Ha! I knew I could get you moving," grinned the rabbit. "I love that trick, love it. Gets 'em every time."

"Well, I don't particularly appreciate it."

"Yeah, pal. Lots of people aren't crazy about it at first. Story of my life. It's a nasty job but somebody's gotta do it. Now listen up, will you? You're lucky because you're already close to where you ought to be. Go through the clearing over there, see? Past the third shecklebush thicket, hang a left along the creek, follow it, and you're there."

"Then I'm *where*?"

"The Grove of Healing. Hey, you need it, pal. Don't tell me you don't. Now don't give me a hard time, okay? Just get over there."

## Grove of Healing

Blesivor entered the Grove of Healing and sat on the soft moss surrounded by tall, leafy ferns, his arms resting on his knees and his head bowed in his arms. He recalled the terrible moment with the rock and spoke it aloud tearfully. The tall ferns moved and swayed and bent to touch him. He felt a lightness and a wholeness he hadn't known for many days.

As he left the Grove of Healing, his companions, including Vopalt, were waiting and smiling. Blesivor knew that the Master had made everything all right again.

It called for a celebration of the Master's presence with them. So they made a very special meal. . . .

---

## Breathtaking reality

You have probably begun to see how the incidents in this fantasy help us to see the wonder of the sacraments. You might even be able to continue the story of the five adventurers through Earthwood to include incidents that remind us of the other sacraments celebrated in the Catholic Church.

Sacraments are a bit unbelievable, just as fantasy stories are a bit beyond the ordinary. We read fantasy because it takes us from our ordinary lives to a world where marvelous things happen, a world where there are special times and special places; where extraordinary, supernatural things happen; where people contact the "other side," the unseen dimension of reality.

For a believing Catholic, the world in which we live is such a world. "Contacting the supernatural" is nothing new. In fact, that can actually be a bit of a problem. We've gotten so used to it that the breathtaking reality has faded and our faith has worn thin.

God has provided ways in which the risen Jesus reaches into our lives, touches us, and changes us. We call them sacraments.

Like our five characters who didn't fully realize what had happened to them at the Crystal Waterfall, we may have forgotten or never really fully understood what our Baptism meant.

At Confirmation we may be deeply affected, as Vopalt and Rea were at the Mountain of Wind and Fire, or it may simply be a very pleasant religious experience as it was for Irin and Skan.

Or, like Blesivor, we may wonder what, if anything, happened. Then we need to rediscover what did happen at the occasion of a sacrament. There's nothing unusual in that. Many people are touched by Jesus without realizing until later, after much reflection and searching, what it truly meant.

When he was on earth, Jesus, our Master, expressed his love to the people he met. In the life of the Church, Jesus continues his love through special actions and sacraments in which he touches and changes us.

Sacraments are as real as Jesus, but they're not magic any more than Jesus was magic. A few thousand years ago in Palestine, Jesus was *there,* available to everyone around him. But not everyone was affected by his presence. He will not grab us, shake us, and change us if we don't want to be changed. Sacraments usually affect us to the degree we are open and willing to be affected.

We don't have to fantasize about meeting Jesus in the sacraments. Meeting him is one "fantasy" that he has made real.

# 5
# Holy This
# and Holy That

Have you ever wanted to be an angel? I don't mean the earthly type — the adorable, practically perfect human being. I mean an *angel* angel, the kind that hangs out in heaven. Wouldn't it be really something to fly great distances in seconds or float around invisibly, spying on friends?

A number of practical things can help you see that being an angel isn't all that great. Swimming is one. Not having bodies, angels never get uncomfortably hot, but neither can they feel the fabulous rush of cold water enveloping them as they dive into a pool. Angels can't ride Space Mountain, the wonderfully wild roller coaster at Disney World. Nor can they feast on pizza or tacos. Angels can't do lots of those things that involve atoms and molecules, things and bodies.

## Special moments and memories

Our lives are full of things, places, times, and bodies. Most of these touch our lives on a fairly ordinary level. A few inches from me right now, for example, are a cassette recorder, a yellow legal pad, and some pens, pencils, and markers. These are helpful and useful things — but not special.

Some of the objects in our lives are special, however. Also a few inches from me in a drawer are a pocketknife and a small, round, red and white fishing float. I took them from the windowsill in my father's apartment the day I found him in a chair, dead from a heart attack he had apparently suffered the previous night. These items weren't usually out on the windowsill so, shortly before he died, my dad must have been thinking about going fishing.

Upstairs in a small wooden box filled with keepsakes, my wife has a plastic label that simply says "NICE." On one of our first dates I punched it out with a label-making device and stuck it on her forehead.

Each of you probably has at least one *special object* like that. It might be a watch that belonged to your father or grandfather, a ring or necklace that belonged to your grandmother, a Christmas tree ornament that carries a special memory. There could be many identical objects in the world that are not special at all. For example, there are literally thousands of fishing floats absolutely identical to the one I keep in a drawer, but only that one is special. You could make millions of "NICE" labels the same size, same color, same everything, but they would not be the same and they would not be special.

There are *special actions* in our lives too. A warm handshake or gesture of affection from someone close to us can be very special. There are also *special words* — a nickname or a phrase with a unique meaning between certain people.

Some *times* are special. Christmas is perhaps the best example. Just being "in" Christmastime does something special for us. And some *places* are special: a favorite part of the backyard, a hide-away corner of the basement, a quiet spot along the shore of a lake or river, a particular bench or swing in the park.

## Staying in touch

Special objects, actions, words, times, and places are special because they put us in touch with people and ideas that are important to us. They refresh our understanding of those ideas and renew our relationship to those people.

On a special wedding anniversary, for example, a couple may want to renew their vows — not just anywhere — but in the church where they were married. They may go on a second honeymoon to the place where they spent their first one. They may order a certain meal, listen to a certain song, or dance a certain dance. All these things (times, places, objects, words, actions) help refresh the idea of their love, renew their promises to each other, and deepen their relationship.

Our Catholic faith is full of things that put us in touch with Jesus and what we believe about him. We have seven major instances in which we literally meet the risen Jesus and contact the source of our Christian life. We call them *sacraments.* Each sacrament involves something very physical, like water, bread and wine, or special words.

There are other special things, not quite as spectacular, that we call sacramentals. That little "al" suffix says it all. You'll remember from English class (OK, so maybe you won't — no problem) that "al" at the end of a word means "sort of like" or "in the manner of."

Sacramentals revolve around the sacraments; they're "sort of like" sacraments. You might compare them to pieces of crystal around a chandelier with a bright bulb in the center. The pieces of crystal don't make the light, but they help bring it to you and help you appreciate it.

Similar to the special times, places, actions, words, and objects that put us in touch with important ideas and people in our daily life, sacramentals are special times, places, actions, words, and objects that put us in touch with Christ and important ideas in our faith life.

Many sacramentals are things that have been blessed for a special purpose. The Catholic Church has a treasury of them: candles, holy water, holy oil, the ashes we receive at the beginning of Lent, the palm that's distributed a week before Easter, scapulars and medals, incense, wedding rings . . . it's a long, long list and this is just a small part of it.

## Using the power of sacramentals

We have to be careful to understand sacramentals correctly. A blessed object is special but it's not magical. It doesn't bring an automatic, no-matter-what result. It is also the case that more is not necessarily better. On Ash Wednesday, if I cover my whole face with ashes and shake some more on my head instead of just wearing a touch on my brow, that won't make me more repentant. Neither will reapplying ashes every three hours every day during Lent.

You might say, by way of example, that a sacramental is like a charged battery. There's power in it, but the power doesn't make anything happen unless something is plugged into it. What gets plugged into and releases the power of a sacramental is our faith, our relationship with Jesus, and our love for God and the Church. Ashes by themselves won't make me repentant — I have to bring my faith and my relationship with Jesus into it.

Let's go back to my dad's fishing float. It's special because it belonged to my dad, but it's not magical. It won't make a school of trophy-sized bass attack my bait. It won't automatically inject me with fishing skills I never had before. But it can help me remember all the neat things my dad taught me about fishing. It can inspire me to adopt more of his enthusiasm, his patience, his cleverness — and in those ways make me a better fisherman. It can help me remember and appreciate the joy of watching the sun come up on a lake as we did together so many times in the past.

That's because he and I already have a relationship. The power in that particular float works in combination with my knowing my dad and believing what he taught me. Someone else who never knew my dad could look at that same fishing float, even use it, and not be affected at all.

Let's relate this to holy water. For someone who doesn't believe in Jesus, holy water is wet and that's about it. That person's lack of faith blocks the power of the blessed water. For the believer, however, holy water is related to the water and the power of Baptism. Does using it with awareness and faith bring about a small renewal, so to speak, of Baptism? Absolutely!

We're dealing with a joining of two things here: the power of the object and the faith of the user. We probably find it simpler to think in terms of an either/or situation: Either the power is all in the object or it's all in the believer's mind. That's really not the way it is, however. If the power were all in the object, we'd have magic. If it were all in the believer's mind, we'd have fantasy.

The action of sacramentals is not either/or. It's a combination of a person's faith and a material thing through which God has chosen to communicate a special blessing and love.

Some sacramentals, such as holy water, are well-known and used universally and often in the Church. Others are less common. Almost any object that can be related to our faith life in some way can become a sacramental through a Church-authorized blessing.

Places can be sacramentals — shrines, for example, and the blessed ground of a cemetery. So can the words of blessings, and actions such as the Sign of the Cross.

Times, particularly the liturgical seasons of Advent, Christmas, Lent, and Easter, can be viewed as sacramentals. You can do penance anytime, but Lent is an especially favorable time for it. During Lent we put a special feeling into the words of the hymn: "This is our accepted time" for penance.

It's probably fantastic being an angel, but since we're not angels, let's appreciate good material things like that wonderfully cool water in the swimming pool and the breathtaking rush of a roller coaster. In particular, let's appreciate and use those times, places, actions, words, and objects called sacramentals . . . God communicating with us, not through a mystical trance but through special things in our material world.

# 6
# Back to the
# Catholic Future

What was it like to be young and Catholic at different times in history?

This may not be a question that's been haunting you day and night for years. Maybe it even reminds you of a horror movie you were forced to watch at school called *The Attack of the Incredibly Disgusting World History Outline.* But let's dig up some stuff from those Great Times of Teenagers Past that can help us think about being young and Catholic today.

## Message for a Roman teen

Did you ever think your parents had gone off the deep end into something totally wild? After all, it's supposed to be the younger generation that gets caught up in far-out stuff. In the second and third centuries, however, many kids must have been convinced that their formerly normal parents (as close to normal as parents can be) had just gotten a good dose of crazy juice.

Take for example TRT, which stands for "Typical Roman Teen." TRT is sixteen and has learned about Jupiter running the cosmic ball park along with all those other powerful gods and goddesses like Neptune and Venus.

TRT doesn't buy the whole Roman god and goddess package, just as many Roman kids (and adults) don't, but TRT figures that part of it might be true. Besides, it's tradition and there is something cool about all those stories of power and mighty deeds.

Then one day TRT's mom and dad come home all turned on saying that Jupiter & Company are a bunch of nobodies. The *real* God, they explain, is the Creator who sent his Son Jesus to save us from sin. Jesus did this by voluntarily sacrificing his life on a cross and then being raised from the dead by God the Father.

"Sure, Mom and Dad. Tell me about it . . . some other time. Right now I've got homework . . . Latin composition. Minimum two-and-a-half pages of loose-leaf papyrus, due tomorrow. Gotta get right on it. Later, okay?"

This is not an easy message for a Roman teenager to understand or accept. As we said, an attractive feature of the Roman gods was the power trip. You hoped that these gods would use their power to turn your enemies into a tasty banquet for a flock of vultures. Then along comes this "new" God saying "Love your enemies . . . forgive those who hurt you. . . . " Well, Mom and Dad have finally flipped!

Can you see any similarities between then and now?

You, too, may not understand where your parents are coming from with their religious beliefs. You, too, live in a world that says, "If you don't like somebody, waste 'em — whether with fists between two people or with bombs between two nations."

So when you think you're watching a home movie called *Mom and Dad Flip Out and Get Hyper About Religious Stuff,* you have something in common with Catholic teens from almost two thousand years ago. The same is true when you feel a conflict between the Christian message of gentleness and peace and a world that worships power.

Remember that a lot of those Roman young people did take the time to consider their parents' new beliefs. They became believers and stayed believers. It's safe to say that they've gone to that Great Racquetball Court in the Sky. So ask them for help as you struggle to accept the teachings of the Catholic Church and the guidance of your parents in religious matters. You don't even have to know their names to make contact.

## Christians versus lions

If you visit Rome, you can check out the Colosseum where, among other real-life violence staged for public entertainment, Christians were put to death. You've probably heard that old warped joke: "The score is Lions 14, Christians 0." Of course that wasn't the final score. The final score shows that the lions have returned to atoms and molecules while the Christians are having an everlasting good time in heaven. God will have to decide the fate of the audience that watched and cheered.

Those Colosseum stories can give you a guilt trip. A little voice says, "*You* don't have to risk anything to be a Christian. Things might be different if you were looking a lion in the face. Would your faith stand up to a challenge like that?"

Well actually, you do have your own Colosseums. You'll find them in school corridors, locker rooms, drive-in movies, and shopping malls. They are the backyards and basements full of too much partying while parents are gone for the weekend. In these Colosseums, the lion's roar sounds like this: "Look, everybody's gonna try to score. Don't be a wimp!" or "Scared of one little joint? Maybe you'd have more fun back home with Mommy and Daddy!"

If you've ever come through pressure like this without giving in, you should feel good about yourself. If you've ever given in but wish you hadn't, or if you're afraid you might, you have some people who can help you. They are the teenage Christians from eighteen centuries ago who listened to the roar of the lions and stayed Christian anyway. You have a lot in common with them. Ask for help and try to follow their courageous example when you face modern-day lions.

## No big deal

In the year 313, the Roman emperor Constantine said, "Retire the lions — Christianity is okay." He became a Christian himself. Now that really says something about the power of Christianity. The mightiest fighting machine the world had ever assembled, after trying for two-and-a-half centuries to wipe out Christianity, was finally saying, "Okay, we give up. In fact, we're joining you."

After that it became easier to be a Christian, teenaged or otherwise. No longer were you asked to risk your life. That, however, can actually be a problem in itself. When it doesn't cost much to belong to something, it's easy not to take it seriously.

Many families had taken great risks and made great sacrifices to live as Christians for several generations. Now it was perfectly acceptable. Kids were born into Christian families. Their baptisms didn't have to be held underground or secretly. So it was easy for a kid to feel, "Well, sure I'm a Christian. No problem. No big deal."

It *is* a big deal. Being a real Christian is always a big deal.

When you start to feel that believing in Jesus is just one of those ordinary things and not a big deal, then your Christian life may be a little like the guy who says, "Sure I believe in exercise. I walk all the way to the TV, then to the refrigerator, and back to the TV a half dozen times every day." In other words, it becomes idle talk with no serious commitment.

If you consider yourself a Christian but it doesn't seem to be costing a darn thing, you may have something in common with those Christians in the decades following Constantine's history-making decision. Anyone in that position should ask the question Christians have always had to ask: "Am I really being a Christian or is it just a label I put on myself?"

## The fall of the Roman Empire

Just as it was easier for a Christian to be a Christian after Constantine, so the people throughout the Roman Empire after the time of Constantine seemed to begin taking things easier and easier. Some historians say the Empire got flabby and out of shape from having everything its own way, from having things too good. This made it a piece of cake for invading barbarians to conquer them.

We'll let historians argue over whether that's the reason or not. In any case, the Roman Empire crumbled under an attack by barbarians. With the fall of the Empire, a lot of things like law and order, government, art, music, science, and literature were also lost from the fabric of society. The invaders didn't know much about any of these things and saw no use for them. (We're talking real crude, uneducated barbarians here, folks, not the Hollywood strongman type of barbarian.)

For quite a while, like several centuries, things were pretty crude. Try living with folks who aren't much different than cavemen, except that they're better armed. (OK, if that describes your brothers and sisters, be grateful for the way they've helped you understand one period of world history.)

Even though life in general was reduced to the basics, being a Christian at that time was complicated and challenging. It's not easy to keep believing in a crucified Savior who preached love when you're living among people who think it's neat to model their lives after some really mean gods named Thor and Wotan. It's not easy to live among people who haven't had your opportunities for education and culture without feeling awfully superior and looking down on them.

And it's particularly not easy to go among them with a message like, "Excuse me, but wasting people with hatchets really isn't nice. And, by the way, how about learning to read some really good books. And incidentally, crude warrior gods like Thor and Wotan are a bunch of nonsense."

The incredible thing is, some Christians did exactly that. Even more incredibly, it worked!

The barbarian invaders didn't change overnight into saintly scholars who walked around reciting the Bible and a complete list of linking verbs. Gradually, however, things got better. In the early ninth century, a man we know as Charlemagne gave a huge boost in that direction by trying to set up something called the Holy Roman Empire. He wanted to get back both the unity and glory of the old Roman Empire and blend it with the Christian faith. He didn't succeed perfectly, but he did awfully well considering that he started with nothing but a dream of a religiously united kingdom.

Thank heaven you don't live among barbarians. Or do you?

"Crude is cool" is the message of a lot of recent concerts and movies.

"Education is stupid!" — well, you just may have met one or two people who think that way.

It's quite possible that you have met some folks who think that breaking things is a kick, and that love and caring and charitable activities are for wimps.

That presents the same three-way challenge it did back in the period of history called the Dark Ages: hanging in with what you know is right, avoiding a "Wow, what animals! God must like me a lot better than these jerks" attitude, and trying to make a difference for the better where you can.

You'll notice that this chapter is coming to an end even though there's a lot of history still to be covered. That's because the next chapter talks about being a Catholic teenager right up through the present time.

Now it's time for a quiz question on all this historical stuff. True or false — Saintly monks who traveled around spreading the gospel formed the Holy *Roamin'* Empire?

# 7
# Back to the
# Catholic Future II

And now, Part II of *The Days of the Lives of All My Catholic Children Who, As the World Turns, Have One Life to Live: Following Jesus, Their Guiding Light, Toward Another World Called Heaven.*

In our previous episode: Almost two thousand years ago, soon-to-be-Catholic teenagers flipped out when their parents came home totally turned on about a Savior who died and then rose again. The young people listened, pondered, and gradually expressed their faith in Jesus. For almost a hundred and fifty years, many got burned at the stake or tossed to the lions because of their beliefs as the Roman Empire tried to wipe out the Christian believers.

In the year 313, an emperor named Constantine made Christianity legal. Now there was a new challenge — to "sell" Christianity to the world without selling out, without blending in too much with the pagan surroundings.

In the fifth century, hordes of really unpleasant dudes known as "barbarians" attacked a fat and lazy Roman Empire, which fell with a huge historical splat. For a while, things were pretty rough and crude. The barbarians acted out "We Don't Need No Education" long before a rock group made it a popular song.

Some Christians had enough courage to attempt educating and preaching to these conquerors. Much to their surprise, they had quite a bit of success. In the year 800, a Christian leader named Charlemagne tried to get everything back together in what he called the *Holy* Roman Empire. He hoped to combine the unity and glory of the old empire with the light of Christian faith.

And now . . . the conclusion of *The Days of. . . .* "

## Good news
## and bad news

Charlemagne's Holy Roman Empire was good news and bad news. The good news was that a lot of little kingdoms that had been trying hard to chop and slice each other up were united. Life became more orderly and more humane due to firm, fair laws. Schools were started so people could learn to read and write. Faith in Jesus spread.

The bad news was that Charlemagne's attempt to blend his political government with the Christian faith was *too* successful. Church government and civil government worked so closely together that sometimes you could hardly tell them apart. Some civil leaders started telling the pope and bishops what to do while some Church leaders started acting like greedy, power-hungry politicians.

Growing up Catholic in those days was more than a little bit confusing. When you couldn't tell your bishop from a politician, it was confusing — and a bad scene. It presented Christians with a special challenge: how to hang onto their faith when some leaders of that faith were being unfaithful.

It was especially a big challenge for the young people. When adults preached one thing but did another, it was difficult to accept their message. It was extremely easy to think, "If *they* don't live up to their ideals, why should I?"

We can learn some valuable things from young Catholics of those times. First, leaders are not perfect. They are human beings who make mistakes. But if you *know* their actions are mistakes, you should learn from that and not go out and make the same ones.

The second lesson that comes from this era is that even if people who preach a true idea don't live up to it, the idea is still true. Those people may even be hoping you won't make the same mistakes. If your dad says "I don't ever want to see you getting drunk!" and you smell a huge dose of bourbon on his breath as he says it, he may honestly be trying to keep you from the hell of alcoholism that he's going through.

## Crusaders for Christ

A second piece of good news/bad news resulted from the close union of Empire and Church. At the end of the tenth century, Moslems (members of the Islamic religion) had gained control of Palestine, the place where Jesus had lived. To say this upset the Christians would be putting it mildly.

The Christians simply had to do something about it — or at least they had to try. Since Christians *are* the Empire and the Empire *is* Christianity, they thought, we'll just get a Christian army together, march on over there, and let those Moslems know who's in charge.

These military campaigns were called the Crusades. Altogether there were eight of them. Growing up Christian during those times was like belonging to a huge vigilante committee out to right a wrong.

Some good things came from these Crusades, but they weren't as totally noble as Christians of the day liked to think they were. It's difficult to find a Scripture passage where Jesus preaches a gospel of "I'm right — you're wrong. Therefore, I'm going to waste you."

There's a lesson to be learned from the action of the Crusaders. Whenever we're defending something we think is right, we have to keep remembering that our goal must be to speak the truth and not try to destroy the individuals who hold another opinion. For example, when you're in a discussion about the evils of abortion or how drugs are bad news, you must be sure that you try to promote the right idea without trying to conquer a person you see as an enemy who deserves to be destroyed.

## Catholic and Christian

So far we've been using the words "Catholic" and "Christian" to describe a single universal group. For centuries that was true. Then, in 1054, Christianity split in two. The Western Church (basically Europe), which came to be known as the Roman Catholic Church, along with some Eastern Catholics from Asia and the Middle East, remained loyal to the pope. The Eastern Church (most Christians in Asia and the Middle East), which came to be known as the Eastern Orthodox Church, gave allegiance to the Bishop of Constantinople. In history this is called "The Great Schism," a fancy phrase indicating separation or division.

Looking back we can see that the disagreements were caused mainly by a lack of communication and by different customs and cultures rather than by great differences in beliefs.

For ordinary people on both sides, especially the younger ones, it was probably no big deal. Perhaps they didn't even know about it until years later. (There were no instant electronic news updates in those days, remember.) Their reaction might have been, "Okay, so those guys don't want to be part of us anymore. Big deal!"

Now we know that the split was tragic. After a separation of nearly a thousand years, each side is beginning to realize how much it can learn from the other and how nice it would have been to share the wealth all along instead of developing separately.

You've probably been through a few smaller schisms yourself. A group of friends splits up and each side bad-mouths the other for a while. Later (maybe a year later, maybe not until a class reunion) you all realize it was dumb and you lost out on what the other group had to offer. By trying to keep your mind open and by being willing to talk honestly, you might keep the next schism from happening.

From this point on you need to realize that "Catholic" does not include *all who believe in Jesus*. The name "Catholic" identifies those Christians who remain united under the leadership of the pope.

## The Black Plague

In my junior year of high school a record number of kids got the flu. More would be absent each day, and still more would leave in the middle of class. In a strange way it was exciting. We kept an unofficial count of how many kids were out and wondered if the school would have to close. Finally it did. For those who didn't get the flu or who recovered quickly, it was great — an unexpected vacation in the middle of the year.

Magnified a few million times over, that's what happened in Europe in the fourteenth century. A lot of schools and businesses closed because of an epidemic. But the epidemic, called the "Black Plague," was not exciting or great. It lasted for fifty years and about one out of every three people in Europe died during that time.

Growing up in that century meant seeing one person after another swell up, grow discolored, and die . . . maybe your mother, your father, brothers or sisters, friends, neighbors . . . and wondering, "How can a loving God allow this to happen?"

At the same time you would have seen people risking their own lives to feed, nurse, and bury victims no one else would get near — all in the name of Jesus. And so maybe you'd decide after all that "a God who can fill people with that much love *must* be real."


## Search for answers

Nearly everybody likes to study. Really! It's just that some people enjoy traditional school things like algebra and literature while others prefer studying non-school things like high-compression engines or gymnastics or wrestling trivia. When you're really into something it's easy to think, "Knowing about this is what *really* counts. Religion is . . . well, it's okay but. . . . "

If you've had that feeling, you know something of what it was like to be a Christian during the age we call the Renaissance: the fourteenth through sixteenth centuries. People got genuinely turned on with learning about their world and thinking about life. They rediscovered the achievements of Greece and Rome. Science and the fine arts flourished.

While the Renaissance was basically a good thing, some people went too far. Their attitude was: "Jesus is okay, but Socrates or Plato have the *real* insights into life. . . . Sure there's a God, but he's nothing to get hyper about. . . . Religion is filled with superstitions. . . . If you want an explanation of what's really going on, study science and find out what can be proven."

Sound familiar?

Unless you're getting a degree in theology, you'll spend far more time studying "other" things than you will studying religion. That's OK. There's a lot to learn about this world. What must be avoided is the attitude that knowing how to run a business is actually more important than knowing right from wrong — or thinking that space technology can provide answers to what life is all about.

## More division in the Church

Think of a time when a group you belonged to split apart. Now there's the smaller group that you are in and the "other guys." Each group considers itself the "original" group.

You want to show the other guys how wrong they are. They feel the same way. You're positive that your side is right. Even when the other guys point out your faults and mistakes and you realize some of what they are saying is true, you still prefer to think about how wrong *they* are.

That's a tiny glimpse of what it was like during the period called the Reformation, the time when the Churches we now call "Protestant" were formed. The reasons for the splits are too complex to talk about here, but we're still feeling and living with the effects of those divisions that began in the sixteenth century. If you don't know how dramatic the divisions were, look up "churches" in the Yellow Pages of the telephone directory. You'll find many different types of Christian churches.

Going back to our example, let's say you believe the other guys are making dangerous changes in the beliefs and practices of your original group. To give your members a solid understanding of "who you are and what you stand for," your group insists that *nothing* ever change. Basically it would be a good idea. Members of your group would be proud to be members. You might, however, start to get a little sensitive and judge everything (both important ideas and small, insignificant ones) simply by whether or not it's "the way you've always done it." That would not be so good.

In time your group stands out because it stayed the same while others changed. People become suspicious of your beliefs. You often get hassled. Sometimes, when you are in the majority, your group does a little hassling of its own.

If you can picture this example, you have an idea of what it was like to grow up Catholic in the period from the Reformation down to very recent times. Unfortunately, we've greatly had to simplify the controversies surrounding the Protestant Reformation.

In fact, we've had to simplify all through this brief look at our history because this was a two-chapter summary and not a two-volume book. History teachers reading this may shake their heads in disbelief and say, "But it's not that simple. You left out the part about. . . . " And they're right. You might be interested in checking out your Catholic history in more detail.

The amazing thing is that we're still here. Things like new computer companies and new television programs and new football leagues start out with high-tech planning and executive geniuses and millions of dollars . . . and then collapse or go bankrupt in a few years (or even months).

Jesus began with a few poor, relatively uneducated people. Two thousand years later, the Christian religion and the Catholic Church are stronger than ever. There can be only one explanation for this.

He is still with us — just as he promised he always would be.

# 8
# Jesus and the
# Materialistic Monster

"And now just when you need it most, Rippem Offanson's Department Store brings you a new wave of exciting products! That's right, folks, just in time for your shopping pleasure, we have restocked our stores with STUFF! We even have STUFF II, III, and IV — the sequels.

"And that's not all! After you have bought lots and lots of STUFF, take a look at our incredible assortment of THINGS! We have just the THING for everyone on your shopping list.

"And don't forget THINGS for yourself! This is 'Be Good to Yourself Week' at Rippem Offanson's. As soon as you enter the store, you'll receive a brightly colored pencil and a special 'Me Want!' note pad. As you browse through the store and see lots of STUFF and dozens of THINGS you want, jot them down on your 'Me Want!' note pad. Give a page or two to each of your friends, tell them to hurry on down to any of our stores, and remind them that they can charge it all! Everybody gets charged up by STUFFing themselves and their loved ones full of THINGS from Rippem Offanson's!"

## Stuff and things

OK, I know it's not that bad. Sometimes it comes close, though. We face this situation every day. Sunday newspapers are packed with advertisements. It is especially bad at Christmas. It's an old battle that might be staged something like this:

"Introducing in the near corner, weighing in at seven pounds three ounces, everyone's sentimental favorite: Jesus, the Real Meaning of Christmas! His opponent in the far corner, weighing in at six hundred and forty-nine pounds: Goliath, the Materialistic Monster."

THINGS — are they good or bad? Actually, they can be either good or bad. In a way, every atom and molecule around us can lead us toward God or away from God, depending on how we use or refuse to use them.

When Mom and Dad buy Johnny a Quadri-Modal Realistic Hyper-Dimension Space Station (action figures and accessories not included) or give Janie a Wet 'N Bawl, Walk 'N Talk, Crawl 'N Roll designer doll (batteries and mini-diapers not included), and when these gifts convey lots of love, then a little bit of Bethlehem has been made present in that house.

On the other hand, when lots and lots of things are *positively expected,* and when Christmas is a huge disappointment if they don't show up beneath the tree, that's a whole different ball game. That's not the kind of life Jesus came to teach us to live.

Still, we live in a material world and we can't get away from stuff and things, even by going to live in a monastery. Let's look at how Christians can best respond to the materialistic cravings fostered by our society.


## The creation of stuff

Several billion years ago God made STUFF; scientists call it matter. About three or four million years ago he made human beings, who were partly stuff and partly spirit. He took a look at it all and said something like "All *right!"* (see Genesis 1:31).

THINGS were supposed to help bring creatures to God and God to creatures. It was a great idea. (Obviously, look who thought of it.) Then along came sin, which is basically a case of people trying to play God and call all the shots.

Sin spoiled the role of things, atoms and molecules, including the ones in human bodies. Because of sin, things tended to draw people away from God rather than toward God. Just look at what folks were already trying to do in Genesis chapter eleven: They piled up atoms and molecules into this tower so they could really get up high and play God. The situation was, to put it mildly, really messed up.

After many generations, Jesus came to earth. He lived, sacrificed his life for us, and rose again. That made everything different. In a nutshell, it is possible once again to live as God intended us to live and to be united with God forever in heaven.

## Using stuff correctly

Since Jesus came to earth, we have a clearer picture of God. Jesus gave us more than a picture, however. He *was* and *is* God in a human form. In a very concrete way, Jesus showed us how God wants people to live together in love, care for the poor and needy, and worship God in prayer and action. Jesus also showed us how God wants us to use the material things of earth, the stuff and the things we see around us everyday.

Jesus could do this in a way we understand because he had a body like us and because he used STUFF: natural objects like water and wood and grain; man-made items like saws and ropes and water jars and boats and fishing nets. He drew pictures in the sand. He made mud with his own saliva.

Because Jesus lived on earth in a human form, THINGS (atoms and molecules) are different now. They can still lead us away from God if we use them only for our own personal comfort or for forbidden pleasures. It's also possible, however, for things to bring us to God and God to us. They can talk to us about God, show us something of God's creative power, and give us a chance to use them for the good of others.

Of course, we have to be attentive to the stuff and the things around us. We also have to be conscious of the right and wrong ways to use material things. Further, we have to be listening to the Word of God as it guides us in the right use of created things.

## Finding God in stuff

Let's look at some of the material things that surround us, the things God has created for us to use properly and enjoy. Remember a time when you walked in a snowfall; remember the feelings you had then. (If you live where it never snows, use your imagination!) Feelings on the outside (the slightly tickly touch of snow on your face and eyelashes) and feelings inside (wow . . . this is different, this is neat, this is really cool to look at and enjoy) both help us to see God's presence in our world.

Because Jesus became human and lived in our material world and was part of it, he made it possible for us to hear and see and touch God through atoms and molecules. An experience of snowfall has the potential to be a message about God. Maybe we heard it, maybe we didn't . . . but it was there.

The wonderfully different feeling of breathing frigid air into our lungs, the neat sound of snow crunching beneath our footsteps, the sheer joy of picking up snow and throwing it somewhere, all of it making an experience that was different, exciting, challenging, and just plain fun . . . that was God saying, "Hey, I want you to think of me when you use the things I have created for you."

Maybe we're not being fair to people in southern regions who seldom experience a really good snowfall. OK, let's do sun — warm, relaxing, cheerful, life-giving. That's also God talking, in this case through the electromagnetic spectrum, as scientists call it, and with the speed of light, if we're aware enough to catch it.

It's not just God talking; it's God giving. We have to be aware to receive both the message and the gift. We can lie in the sun and just get a suntan or we can lie in the sun and get both a tan and the awareness of being surrounded, filled, warmed, and loved by God. Depends on how open we are to God.

## Given with love

We need to consider both the material things that God gives to us and the way we choose to use those material things for our own good and for the good of other people.

Let's say you're sitting at a restaurant counter, about to chomp into your double cheeseburger. You'd really like some catsup because you enjoy extra catsup on your double cheeseburger. Now if somebody sitting next to you sets a catsup bottle down where you can reach it, well, that might be just an accident or maybe the person is simply being an OK human being and thinks it's the correct thing to do, figuring you'd ask for it sooner or later anyway.

On the other hand, if your best friend sets the catsup bottle down next to you, it's the same action with a different meaning. This person *knows* you like catsup on your double cheeseburger and you know this person knows it. Giving you the catsup bottle is no accident. You can tell that this is your friend's way of saying, "I care about you and I want to make you happy. So here's your catsup . . . have a ball drowning your double cheeseburger in it."

That's the way it is with us who believe in God and in Jesus who was born in Bethlehem, a human being who blessed stuff and things by using them himself, who made them able to talk to us about God, and who also made us able to listen. We see and feel the snow, the sun, the rain, the wind, and all kinds of things, and we know these are gifts because we know who made them and sent them.

Sometimes even not having things can be a message. If you're sitting at a restaurant counter and a stranger takes the saltshaker out of your reach, you might say there's a mean dude that doesn't like you or people in general. But if your mother moves the salt-shaker out of your reach, again it's the same action with a different meaning. She knows you use more salt than is good for you and she's trying to keep you from harming your health.

## Using things wisely

God isn't too difficult to find in things like snow and sun and rain and wind. What about the stuff and things from Rippem Offanson's where we began this chapter? When Jesus blessed material creation by being part of it, did he include all the plastic and polyester? Does God send us messages through the gadgets that are on sale this weekend at only twenty-five percent off?

Depends. That's not a cop out answer. It really does depend on how we use the fancy gimmicks and gadgets that technology has made possible. We can use a VCR to watch great films or we can use it to watch pornography.

It also depends on how attached we get to stuff, how much we want to grab it all and keep it for ourselves. When that happens, the atoms and molecules are keeping us distant from God instead of leading us toward him.

If I'm overly concerned about getting lots and lots of material things for myself, and if I'm stuck on how incredibly cool I am because I have all the latest stuff to wear and look at and listen to and ride in and show off and be entertained by . . . well, it's going to be awfully difficult for God to contact me through those things or for those things to help bring me to God.

On the other hand, if I share the things I have with others and if I use some of my allowance and salary to help others obtain the material things they need to survive, then I am aware of God speaking to me through the things of earth. I show by my actions that I have heard the Word of God and been influenced by the example of Jesus.

# 9
# Afterlife I

Do you ever wonder about a relative or friend who has died? Do you wonder about what they are experiencing? Do you ever find yourself wanting to know if eternity is really the way artists picture it or preachers talk about it?

Those who have died know from experience what happens "over there," on the "other side," after death. Unfortunately, they are quite unable to communicate their experiences to us.

You may feel that a discussion of "after death" is about as practical as a story on famous landmarks of Antarctica. You probably think that you are going to be around for so many more years that it is silly and morbid to think about death and the afterlife at this point in your life.

Remember, there's no life-span guarantee for anybody. Even if you have sixty more birthday cakes to cut or seventy more Christmas trees to decorate, you probably wonder sometimes about what there will be for you when the birthday cakes and Christmas trees finally run out.

It's something we should think about because eternal life is at the very core of the Christian message. The apostles didn't go around saying, "May we have your attention, please. Here are a set of principles regarding faith and morality around which you should structure your daily actions." That came later and it's important, but it's not the headline of the story. A big part of the basic Christian message was (and still is): "Hey, folks, we're going to live *forever!*"

The first obvious questions are "Where?" and "What's it going to be like?"

## Faith, not physics

We don't have news bulletins or on-the-scene reports from the next world. "Good evening. This is your friendly eyewitness news reporter speaking live from heaven. The singing you hear in the background. . . . " Anyone who expects religion to come up with graphic, detailed descriptions and analyses of eternity is going to be disappointed. What we know about heaven, hell, and purgatory comes from Scripture and Church tradition — and that means *faith*, not physics.

"How do you know it's like that?" is a decent question to ask in biology or chemistry. You can expect an answer based on what people have actually observed or mathematically proven.

"How do you know?" is a valid question to ask in religion too. Just remember that here we're dealing with something that's often way too big to fit into our minds. Sometimes the answers make perfect sense. Other times there's an answer, but we can't completely figure it out until we get a little mental click and we say, "Oh yeah, now I get it!" Still other times the only answer is, "We don't know."

When that happens some people say, "If religion can't come up with a better answer than that, I'm not buying into it." (Strangely enough, some of these same people have no problem at all accepting extraterrestrials and horoscopes and a lot of other things they will never be able to prove.

Here's what our faith teaches about life after death.

## Looking toward forever

In a way we can say that the afterlife comes in two stages. The first stage lasts from the time of your death until the end of the world. The second stage lasts from the end of time until . . . well, there is no more until. From then on it's forever.

We humans are a hybrid, so to speak. We're partly matter (our bodies) and partly spirit (our soul). The soul is the thinking, choosing, loving aspect of us, although in this life we often use our bodies to carry out those feelings, thoughts, and decisions.

At death, the body crumbles back into atoms regardless of what we may have rubbed, painted, or sprayed on it while it was alive. The soul doesn't have any matter to crumble. It begins to exist apart from the body and no longer depends on the body. It is the soul or spirit of a person that lives on in eternity and experiences and knows the joy or sadness of life with God or life apart from God.

Eternity presents each person with several possibilities. One is heaven. That isn't too hard to take, although to many people heaven doesn't sound like a big turn-on and may even sound a little boring. That's because of our limited vision of heaven, our narrow interpretation of "seeing God." The other possible experiences of afterlife are referred to as "purgatory" and "hell."

## 'Twixt heaven and hell

Purgatory is a confusing idea to many non-Catholics who find it difficult or impossible to accept. Even Catholics who have heard about it since they were children have trouble understanding what it will be like.

Traditionally we've learned that purgatory is a place of temporary punishment for sin. Souls in purgatory are assured of making it to heaven, but first they have to be cleansed or purified of the sinfulness that was present in their lives at the time of their death. This sinfulness and separation from the ways of God wasn't bad enough to send them to hell but it was enough to keep them from immediately entering heaven.

There are few specific references to purgatory in Scripture, but check out the Second Book of Maccabees, chapter twelve. People fighting under the Israelite leader Judas (not the apostle-betrayer Judas) had given their lives fighting for the Lord. When their bodies were being gathered for burial, they were found to be wearing charms dedicated to pagan gods. In other words, they ended up with a mixed bag of good and evil.

Judas ordered prayers said and sacrifices made on behalf of those who died in order to make up for their sins. The Bible specifically stated that this was a good thing to do.

This passage contains two elements of the Catholic view of the afterlife: After death we don't necessarily go immediately to heaven or hell; and there's a mysterious connectedness between people who have died and people who are still living. Because of this connectedness, we can affect one another across the borderline of this world and the next.

Other Christian faiths see life after death as an immediate either/or situation. You either find salvation during your life or you don't, and you experience the results (heaven or hell) as soon as you die.

To them, the idea of God deliberately making people wait and suffer for a while and then, after a certain point, welcoming them into heavenly happiness doesn't make sense. In fact, the picture can seem a bit odd: Joe Earthling is in purgatory suffering the pain of separation from God. God looks at him and says, "Don't you wish you hadn't screwed up, Joe? This will teach you. You just stay there and suffer some more." Joe stays there feeling bad about his mistakes and upset that he is not enjoying heaven with God. Then suddenly God says, "Okay, I'm satisfied," and he brings Joe to heaven, throws his arms around him, and says, "I really love you, Joe. Welcome to heaven."

## Getting into shape

We can look at purgatory another way.

Imagine a coach who gives his or her players a fitness program to follow, a set of plays to study, a curfew, and some other rules to keep — all for their own good and the good of the team. If they follow the rules, work off any flab, get themselves into shape, sharpen their coordination, and learn what to do in various situations, they'll be guaranteed playing time.

OK, the season is starting. Here's Player Number One. He or she follows the coach's program and shows up physically fit and ready to play. So the coach sends Player Number One into the game right away.

Player Number Two messes up. He or she is not a physical disaster, but not an athlete either: broke curfew a few times, didn't get enough exercise, is a little fuzzy on some of the play patterns. It's not a hopeless case. Player Number Two doesn't deserve to be kicked off the team, but he or she is not really ready to play.

So the coach says, "I'll keep you on the team but I can't put you in the game. You're simply not ready to play yet. I'll put you on a crash training program. It won't be fun, but it will get you in shape to play."

The crash training program includes some pretty tough stuff in the way of diet, exercise, and study. It'll hurt. When flabby muscles are exercised, they hurt. That's just the way it is. But it's a good hurt. It's a sign that needed conditioning is taking place. The coach isn't giving this crash training program purely as a punishment or because he or she enjoys watching a player suffer. It's simply necessary in order to get the player ready for the real game.

Many of us are like Player Number Two when we finish our time on earth. We're not dripping with raw evil, but we're not quite ready to play in the heavenly game either.

Heaven is a place of total loving. You have to be a completely loving person to function there. If we have some unloving, sinful selfishness left in us, it's like flab that needs to be toned up and worked out of our systems.

That's what happens in purgatory. The word itself comes from the word *purge,* which means "to get rid of."

What exactly is purgatory? We don't know. It probably isn't fire as we know it (despite all the pictures you might have seen) because spirits or souls can't be affected by temperature. Whatever it is, no doubt it hurts because God is absent. It probably hurts in the same way that it hurts when you are separated from someone you love a lot.

If you talk to people going through a period of temporary separation, you will find more than simply the pain of absence, loss, and emptiness. Many of them also experience an exciting, hopeful feeling, even a positive high. They know that even though the separation hurts, it is not forever and they will soon be on the way to being reunited, to being together again.

## Reaching out to the deceased

I mentioned a mysterious connectedness between us and the souls of those who have died. We are able to affect each other's lives. How this works is not completely clear, but our tradition has always taught that we can help the souls in purgatory through our prayers — and they can help us with their suffering. Souls in heaven don't need any help, of course, but we can certainly ask for theirs.

What if somebody dies and happens to have fifty friends and relatives praying like crazy for him or her, while somebody else dies and nobody knows or cares? Will that first person get a spot in purgatory's express lane while the second one waits practically forever?

I don't think so. I don't know exactly how God makes it work out evenly, but I believe he does. It may be frustrating not to know "how it all works," but it does. If you believe in a God of love, you have to believe in a God who in the next life is completely just and merciful!

# 10
# Afterlife II

In the previous chapter, we established that when it's all over, it's *not* all over. You will never be "all over." After death, but before the end of time, there's the possibility of heaven, of purgatory, and . . . well, the final possibility is one hell of an idea, but not in a good sense.

Actually, hell is a rotten idea — so rotten we hate to think about it. We love to say, "I just can't believe a loving God would send anybody to such a place." It's tempting because it gets us off the hook.

Unfortunately, that opinion goes against many things that Jesus said very plainly. It goes flatly against dozens of things in the New Testament.

How can we make sense of hell in terms of an all-loving God? The example of the coach we used in the previous chapter will help again; this time with Player Number Three.

Player Number Three shows up for the season a complete physical and mental wreck. He has done almost nothing but party and goof off all through training: late hours; sometimes too little sleep, sometimes too much; nonstop junk food; almost no time given to studying the plays; huge doses of booze, pot, pills, drugs — you name it. The result is a burned-out mind that can't think straight or remember much, and a body so shot it can't even walk decently, much less move athletically.

The coach has no choice but to say, "You're off the team." It's not purely a punishment. It's a fair decision because the player has made himself or herself permanently unable to function in the game. The coach probably feels awful about the whole thing because he or she really likes that kid. The coach might burst into tears and say, "How could you do this to yourself? You had such a great future. I had such terrific plans for you."

That doesn't change matters. The kid can't play, won't ever be able to play, and did this to himself or herself.

## Losing out

What's it like in hell?

It's the complete cosmic opposite of heaven. Since we haven't experienced heaven yet, we'll have to give an example using material things. Now material things don't guarantee true happiness and joy, but in this life they often impress us and they can help illustrate a point.

Imagine that your incredibly rich uncle plans to give you five billion dollars. That's right: *five billion dollars!* He wants to give it to you next Saturday evening at 8:00 p.m. It's now Sunday morning.

Five billion dollars. There's almost nothing in the world you couldn't buy with that much money!

You don't have to take a test or do anything extraordinary to earn it. It's purely a gift. The check is already made out in your name. Your uncle simply asks that you show your gratitude by being a generous, giving, sharing person. Sometime during this week he wants you to give ten hours of service to other people.

Now ten hours of service is going to take a little effort, but compared with the gift, it's a piece of cake.

You figure there's no sense starting on Sunday. Sunday is supposed to be a day off, right? There's plenty of time.

On Monday some friends ask you to a movie, so you go. Afterward they want to stop for a pizza. You want to tell them that you can't, that you need to be giving service to people because five billion dollars is at stake. Since you know they won't believe that, you stay with them.

On Tuesday the group is going to the mall. You go with them because they're your friends. At the mall you see a lost kid, a lady with a flat tire, and a man who's having trouble reading the fine print on a piece of paper. You'd like to stop and help them, but what would your friends think? They'd call you a goody-goody, and you can't afford that. Besides, there's lots of time left in the week.

Wednesday is just loaded with good TV shows.

On Thursday you're in a bad mood and don't feel like helping anybody. You spend a lot of time reading old magazines and complaining on the telephone to your friends about what a stupid world it is.

Friday comes and you're feeling good because it's the end of the week, but who can get into serious stuff on a Friday, for heaven's sake? Besides, you only need ten hours, and there's still tomorrow.

Friday night's party leaves you pretty blitzed. When you wake up, it's 1:30 p.m. Saturday afternoon, and you don't feel like handling anything more than breathing and blinking.

Well, what the heck. Ten hours of service — what's that got to do with being a multibillionaire? Anybody who's nice enough to consider dropping five billion dollars your way is also nice enough not to get upset because you didn't do a few picky little things, right?

You show up at your uncle's on Saturday evening just in time to see the check, made out to you for five billion dollars, float down into the fireplace and turn to ashes.

"I don't understand," your uncle says, deeply hurt and upset. "I wanted you to have that, and it was so simple."

"You mean I don't get the money?"

"You didn't begin to try. You didn't even come close. I'm sorry."

There's almost no words to describe the feeling you'd have, the condition you'd be in right then. Five billion dollars! It could have been yours so easily!

Nearly anything in the world could have been yours; something new and spectacular every day for the rest of your life. You could have had both the fun of enjoying neat things and the joy of sharing them and giving them away. You could have shared your treasure with anyone you met and made them happy. You would have had so much it would never run out.

For what did you trade it all away? For a movie, a few TV shows, acceptance in a group that probably won't be together in a couple of years, a few laughs, and a party that left you exhausted and aching. You traded five billion dollars for a lot of stuff that isn't worth the price of a pound of cardboard.

Have you ever been so angry at yourself that you actually hit yourself or pounded a wall or deliberately broke something you owned, needed, and liked? Take that feeling and multiply it a few billion times. Because you hate yourself so much, you hate everything and everyone around you. You want to break and hurt and destroy everything you see.

Actually, there's a word for that feeling, that condition. . . . The word is *hell*.


## When tomorrow comes no more

There will be a time when planet Earth will have taken the last spin on its tired old axis. Even if the human race migrates from Earth to the outer reaches of the galaxy, there will be a day that won't be followed by another day. In any case, whether it's May 1995 or September 17354, there will be a day without a tomorrow as we know it.

At this point, Church teachings indicate that only heaven and hell will exist. Purgatory's job will have been completed. Two main events are scheduled at this point: the resurrection of the body ("That Great Gettin'-Up Mornin'!" in the words of an old spiritual) and the final judgment.

The latter is simpler to understand. Probably no surprises here. We've already created our destiny. The final judgment is like a permanent lamination of our citizenship papers in heaven or hell.

The resurrection of the body raises more questions and opens up a lot of interesting guesswork.

*Will it happen?* You better believe that it will happen. As with hell, to believe otherwise you'd have to toss out a lot of the New Testament. Jesus himself confronted a group called the Sadducees who did not believe in bodily resurrection, and he told them bluntly they were wrong (see Mark 12:18-27).

*How will it happen?* Your magnificent body will have broken down into tiny pieces of matter. Parts of it may have been recycled to help create award-winning geraniums. If an earthquake rattled your cemetery or if a meteorite landed on your grave, your atoms may be scattered worldwide. How is God going to reassemble them into a bodily form?

He can handle it.

Sorry if you were looking for a more detailed answer, but that's all we have. When you think of it, that's good enough. If God can create this whole cosmic ball park out of nothing, he can certainly handle fashioning some atoms for your resurrected body. It's his problem anyway. Sometimes we worry about more than we need to and try to figure out stuff that isn't our problem. If you believe the resurrection is going to happen, let God handle the nuts and bolts of it.

*What will these resurrected bodies look like? Will the citizens of heaven have heavenly-to-look-at bodies while people in hell gross each other out forever?* That sounds logical, but God hasn't told us.

*Will we look twenty-one or thirty-five or the age we died or what?* We don't know. The New Testament gives us many statements to assure us that the resurrection is going to happen. It also connects our bodily resurrection to the Resurrection of Jesus. Unfortunately, it offers only a few ideas about what the scene will be like when it happens. Most of these are in First Corinthians, chapter fifteen, and even they are not crystal clear.

## Eternal life and joy

What should be clear to you is this: The five-billion-dollar example we used a while ago is nothing compared to the gift God has waiting for you. Don't read past that too quickly; think about it. Five billion dollars and all the stuff you could do with it . . . and it's nothing compared to what God has waiting for you in heaven.

If you have doubts about whether you're worthy of such a reward, you're right. You're not! Nobody is. We don't earn heaven. It's pure gift, not salary. Jesus came, died, and rose again to break the power of death and sin. Because he rose to a new and eternal life, we can too.

All we have to do is cooperate with God and the grace that is offered to us. All we have to do is look beyond the small, temporary, sinful stuff of this life and open our arms to receive God's gift of eternal life and joy.

CPSIA information can be obtained
at www.ICGtesting.com
Printed in the USA
FFOW05n0952090215

9 780892 432714